The
People
Management
HANDBOOK

CHAD HALVORSON

Introduction

The best-kept secret and hardest lesson that no one tells you when you become a manager of people is this: you don't become a great manager overnight—you have to work at it just like anything else you want to excel at. You can't expect to instantly know everything there is to know about managing people just because you were given a piece of paper, a title change, or a salary increase—and no one expects that of you right away.

Most experienced leaders understand that becoming a good manager of people takes practice, perseverance, and commitment. They know that it's not about bossing people around all the time, nor is it about being everyone's best friend. It's not about being stuck in the back office crunching numbers all day (at least it doesn't have to be), and it's not about shucking all your responsibilities onto the people below you.

Managing people is about inspiring people to do their best work. It's about being a good listener, an effective communicator, an idea person, an organized planner, a doer, a finder of great talent, and a person who knows how to make tough decisions when tough decisions need to be made.

I wrote this book, not because I'm perfect or because I have all the answers, but because I've learned a lot in my experience and time as a manager. My hope is that you can use pieces of this book—the lessons I've learned along the way—to become a better manager and leader at your own business. I hope it inspires you to do more for your team, not because anyone tells you that you need to be better, but because it's what your employees deserve.

To build a better team from the ground up, you have to start from the top. This book will help you get started.

Thank you for reading,

Chad Halvorson

CEO of When I Work

CHAPTER 1

The Management Skills You Need To Lead Your Team

Leading a team is every kid's dream. Who doesn't want to be the hero that slays the enemy, gets the gold, and ultimately leads their people to success? But, the reality of leadership isn't like the movies—it's a lot more complicated.

Each team member has a different communication style, and brings a unique skill set to the table. The company has tons of different goals, and it's hard to prioritize what needs to get done, and who needs to do it.

In order to be an effective leader, you need more than a good attitude and a little kid's dream. You need good management skills. Here's my comprehensive list of skills that you'll need to thrive as a manager:

Vision

Where is your company going? What about your team? How do you harmonize the team with the company's goals? Leaders often have the best intentions, but they get caught up in day-to-day management, putting out fires instead of working to unite their people under a shared vision.

Lack of direction leaves team members feeling confused about purpose. They know they're working hard, but it's difficult for them to see their impact. They don't know which initiatives to prioritize. As a leader, you not only need a clear vision, but you also need to communicate it well.

How to get it: If you're struggling to create and communicate your long term vision, step back and think about what that vision is. If you're in middle management, meet with the people above you to help you understand big picture goals. If you're on top, step back and write down a plan. Too many leaders fly by the seat of their pants without assessing goals on monthly, quarterly, and yearly basis.

Effective Communication

Communication is a dirty word. It gets thrown around by people who are unsure of what it really means. At its core, communication is about expressing yourself so that the things you think and the things you say are closely aligned. Communication is the keystone of effective leadership.

You need to communicate:

- Priorities
- Long term goals
- Gratitude
- Strategy and executional information

How to get it: If you feel like you're not a great communicator, try putting things in writing. Plan what you're going to say before a meeting– don't just wing it.

Organization

When we think about being organized, we envision a clean workspace and color-coded post it notes, but organization extends to executional items such as project timelines. Organization is easy for some, impossible for others. Thankfully, there are tools available to help all of us–Gantt charts, excel spreadsheets, project management software (such as Trello and Teamwork) are just a few options.

How to get it: Struggling to keep things together? Papers flying everywhere? Email inbox overloaded? Sit down with someone who is organized and have them help you set up systems. Once you have systems in place, you'll be better able to stay organized and keep your team on the same page.

Functional Skills

It's hard to respect management who can't get stuff done. Someone who can't "do" is problematic– it's like having a ship captain who never learned how to sail. If a leader doesn't have the skill set to understand the industry, and the ability to make things happen, they're probably not a great leader. This doesn't mean that leaders need to be knee deep in the nitty-gritty– instead, they need to effectively delegate and create timelines to ensure that goals are met on time and with quality results.

How to get it: Take a class on leadership and management, or other courses that focus on the functional skills you lack. Find a good, in-person class in your region that focuses on skills such as delegation, difficult conversation, and project timelines. I recommend General Assembly.

Confidence

You're the boss, so you can't let yourself get used by your staff. Confidence is not just a trait– it's also a practiced skill. Confidence comes from knowing yourself well. If you understand your strengths, you can leverage them for success. You can be transparent with your team when it comes to your weaknesses, asking for help so you can move along.

How to get it: Take a personality test. I love Myers-Briggs and DISC assessments. These will help you understand your strengths and weaknesses in an objective way. I also recommend doing things outside your comfort zone. If you're a quiet person, take an improv class. If you're loud, meditate.

Fairness

Nothing frustrates employees more than blatant favoritism. Sure, there will be members of your team that you like more than others, but expressing your true feelings is poison to a team who has to come together. Favoritism is juvenile, and it can poison a team. It's a dagger into camaraderie– so don't pick favorites!

How to get it: If you really favor some team members more than others, you need to create boundaries to put your professionalism in check. When you go out to lunch, invite everyone, not just the guy whose jokes you like. As a manager, you need to make professional friends and contacts, not BFFs.

Respect

Being a good leader doesn't mean getting everyone to unanimously nod their heads every time you open your mouth. Disagreements are inevitable, but a good leader can treat others with respect and kindness, no matter the situation. Ask your reports why they think what they think. Respect their opinions, even if you vehemently disagree. If they do something serious that needs to be addressed, talk to them like they are adults instead of cornering and lecturing them.

How to get it: This one's tough, because we can't help but be hot-headed sometimes. If you feel yourself getting angry in a meeting, take a deep breath, walk out the door, and take a break. Time will calm you down so that when you do discuss hot button issues, you can do so with respect.

Adaptability

Change is the only constant in our lives, and teams look to their leaders when the seas get stormy and the caves get dark. As a leader, you have to adapt. You can't be the one acting like an ostrich, head in the ground, unwilling to accept the changes. The best leader take changes in stride, thriving in transition.

How to get it: When changes come, force yourself to be optimistic, even if you're worried. Connect with the right people, but honest about your skepticism, and be ready to change how you go about things. When someone suggests leading meetings in a new way, don't balk. Carefully consider why you feel the way you do, and be open-minded about a new way of doing things.

Ability to Think Strategically

It's frustrating to work at a place where the leaders take on itty bitty projects without a lot of strategy. They talk to us off the cuff, without thinking about how they come off. We look to leaders for guidance on everything, and when we feel that they're not being deliberate, we panic. Basically, people want to see that you can pull through. How are you going to do what you've said you will do? You must be able to think and act strategically in order to be successful as a leader.

How to get it: According to the *Harvard Business Review*, people lack strategy because they're not taking the time to reflect. Build strategic time into your work day. You need time to reflect on situations so that you can connect ideas together to show your team you can make things happen.

Team Orientation

Yes, you're a leader, but you're also a team member. You are not Michael Jordan— you are the leader of the Chicago Bulls. You have to think like a team member, and always put the team before your own needs. Sometimes that means taking flack for a team member's mistakes, or going to bat when a report asks for a promotion or more compensation.

How to get it: Think of yourself as a team member before thinking of yourself as a leader. Be willing to do things you dislike for the sake of the team. Never act like you're better than your team members just because you're in a position of power.

Navigation of Difficult Conversations

Stressful conversations are inevitable. Laying someone off, talking about an an issue that came up in the office, or critiquing bad performance—all these cause a lot of stress. Leaders are good at having these conversations. They can speak with grace, ask for input, and make people feel like they're safe, even when the content is difficult.

How to get it: Read *Taking The Stress Out of Stressful Conversations* by Holly Weeks from Harvard Business School. Holly outlines how to navigate the stormy territory of tough talk.

Being a manager is hard – there are so many skills you need to be successful. Thankfully, with a little bit of elbow grease, you'll be able to work on these skills to become the best leader in your organization.

CHAPTER 2

How To Write An Effective Employee Handbook

What if there was one tool that could keep all of your employees on the same page, knowing exactly what you expected from them?

That's exactly what an employee handbook does. Your handbook is your uniform message and your all-purpose tool.

It helps you avoid miscommunication with your team by laying out in clear terms what your business is about and what you expect from employees. It gives every employee the same foundational understanding of what your business is all about. It gives employees a place to turn when they have questions and need guidance on what to do when situations arise in the workplace. It provides legal protections for both you and your employee.

Yet many businesses don't have an employee handbook. What's their excuse?

- They think they are too small and don't have enough employees to justify a handbook.
- They don't have anyone with the skills to write one.
- They don't want to spend money for an attorney or HR specialist to help create one.
- They think it will hurt the casual and "pleasant" small-time feel of their business.
- They want to allow managers the ability to interpret policy rather than have it written in stone.

Those sound like good reasons, right? But they're not. An employee handbook both protects you and your employees when things in the workplace get difficult. Here are some tips to get you started.

What To Include In The Handbook

An employee handbook covers the obvious, the seemingly mundane, legal requirements, and the tricky behavior issues, all at once.

Who you are.

Start your employee handbook with an introduction to you and your business. Let employees know a brief history, and understand who you are and what you're all about. This is where you will share your business philosophy and culture.

Work, pay, and benefits.

The next sections of your employee handbook will outline the things employees are generally most interested in (which is why you put them at the start of the handbook).

Hours: Provide details on expectations for both full-time and part-time employees when it comes to the hours worked. Let employees know about overtime, including who is eligible for it and how they go about getting compensation for it.

Pay: Share all information on pay for hourly, salaried, full-time, and part-time employees. Include information on things like bonuses, such as how employees can earn a bonus, or the circumstances through which bonuses are distributed. Talk about pay increases, and when and how that occurs. Let employees know that you will be making the necessary federal and state tax deductions so that they understand the difference between their stated pay and their take-home pay. And don't forget to tell them how often and when they will be paid! Employees need to know when they are to expect their paycheck.

General employment: Talk about any employee referral programs that you might offer, as well as topics such as how and when you post new jobs, termination and resignation policies

Benefits and leave: Lay out the details of the benefits your full-time and part-time employees are eligible for. This includes things like health insurance, retirement, and vacation, but also the rules and guidelines for sick leave and vacation pay. You likely have official documents regarding many of these benefits (e.g. health insurance) from these outside providers, so be sure to refer your employees to these documents, and be sure to make these documents available to your employees. You don't have to include these outside documents in full in your employee handbook.

You should also inform employees of leave policies in regards to military service, disability, crime victims leave, voting leave, bereavement leave and so on. In other words, if you have a leave policy, write it down clearly and let employees know what it involves. Be sure you comply with any laws regarding leave.

Legally required information.

There are some topics you must include in your employee handbook, as required by law. These include:

Family medical leave policies: The Family Medical Leave Act requires that employers, depending on the size of their business, provide up to 12 weeks of unpaid leave during a 12-month time period for the birth or care of a child, or for serious health issues of the employee or a family member they must care for. Your state may have additional requirements, too.

Non-discrimination policies: Each state has their own laws regarding discrimination and equal-opportunity employment, but the federal government also lays out some laws, too. Your handbook should reflect both of these as well as refer employees to applicable legal information provided by the federal and state government.

Workers compensation: Workers compensation policies, according to state and federal law, should be clearly outlined, as well as what employees should do to claim compensation.

Safety issues.

Safety issues range from physical safety using tools and machines at work to personal and emotional safety in the workplace.

Drug and alcohol use: Many workplaces have policies regarding drug and alcohol use, some of which include drug testing. Be sure to clarify what employees are allowed to do both to avoid losing their job (e.g. no illegal drug use) as well as what they should avoid while on duty (e.g. no alcohol while on duty). You will probably want to include a smoking policy; some cities and states have laws that prohibit smoking in the workplace. Be sure to comply with these laws.

Safety: You already know you need to comply with OSHA standards, but outlining your safety policies and approach is wise. Both explain your policy as well as provide instructions for employees to report unsafe incidents so that they are dealt with. Safety information ranges from equipment use to what to do when there is dangerous weather and employees are either at work or can't get to work.

Harassment: Policies regarding harassment include sexual, verbal, bullying, or electronic. This also includes a discussion on being civil to each other in the workplace, and not instigating problems among other employees. Establish your no-tolerance policy for harassment, explain what harassment is, and let employees know what they are to do if they've been harassed.

Complaint Procedures: You will want to include instructions for what employees are to do if they have a complaint. By not allowing for a procedure to handle complaints, you open yourself up to the problem growing bigger, possibly into harassment, and exposing yourself to legal problems. Be clear that no employee will face retaliation for bringing a complaint to management, and instruct them on what to do with their complaints to start the official process.

Your expectations.

Discuss what you expect from your employees regarding work schedules, requesting time off or vacation, and punctuality. You will also want to address daily breaks, meal breaks, dress code, language use. Let them know what standards you expect from your team in terms of honesty, customer service, and fellow employee cooperation.

Computer and internet use: A category many employers don't think to cover is what you expect from employees as far as computer and mobile phone usage. Do you have policies on personal use of mobile phones or work computers while at work and on the clock? Are there security issues that need to be addressed in regards to computer use? What about public relations, and how employees behave on social media or other public-facing accounts that customers could find? Computer and internet use (and abuse) are important to address, depending upon what type of business you run.

NDNA and conflict of interest: Depending on your business, you may require your employees to sign a non-disclosure agreement (NDNA). Explain any conflict of interest policies you have, and what constitutes a violation of these policies.

Disciplinary actions: Part of laying out what you expect is letting employees know that there will be discipline when these expectations are not met. However, avoid the temptation to go into too much detail in this section. The more detail you provide, the more likely it is you'll leave something out.

If your approach is more general, then it will actually cover a broader range and give you the flexibility to address issues rather than if you attempted to outline every single possibility. Progressive discipline often works in most cases, but there are times you need to fire an employee as soon as possible. It's best to make it clear that breaking rules and policies will result in a disciplinary process, but not lock yourself into too much detail.

Caveats.

It is important to note in your handbook that the document is not a contract promising continued employment (more on that next). Instead, it is a handbook that is the final say regardless of any previous documents on policies.

You should also note that policies are subject to change and that there may be additional behaviors not expressly mentioned in your handbook that are subject to what's laid out in your handbook; you can't possibly predict what future issues might arise that need to be addressed, so including this gives you some leeway to act.

What To Leave Out

There are some things you ought to leave out of your employee handbook according to *HR Daily Advisor*, because they can get you into trouble when drafting your handbook. Here are some phrases to avoid using:

Just cause. Not every state has the same legal requirements. At-will states do not require employers to have a cause or reason to terminate or discipline an employee, so including language such as "just cause" in your employee handbook makes things difficult and confusing for you.

Permanent position. Never use the phrase "permanent position", because it suggests to employees that their position is a sure thing when it is not. Again, this ties into the idea of "at will."

Due process. Avoid make reference to "due process" in regards to disciplinary action or in handling employee disputes. Again, you're making things more difficult for you than you are required to. Outlining a rigid disciplinary process that must be followed every time means you may have difficulty firing an employee who truly needs to go as soon as possible without dragging out the process. Always allow yourself the option to fire at will as much as you are legally allowed.

Probationary period. As an employer, you may think of an employe starting off as being in a probationary period, but that language creates the expectation for the employee that once that time is over, they are permanent. Using "introductory" is better language, since it allows for the idea that employees are still employed "at will."

Get A Legal Review

As you can see, simple phraseology or language can get you into trouble that you didn't expect, so have your completed employee handbook reviewed by your attorney before putting it to use. Or, contact an attorney with specialized skill or knowledge in HR or the workplace.

While it will cost you, it is a necessary expense. Your attorney can tell you if the language is appropriate, and if the policies you've outlined in your handbook are within legal bounds. If your business operates in several different states, you may need to adjust your employee handbook to meet the laws of each state. Because your employee handbook might be pivotal in any future issues with employees, it is imperative that you make certain the language that you use legally protects yourself or other employees.

Distribute The Employee Handbook

Now that you have your employee handbook written, put it to work.

An employee handbook must be distributed to each employee in order to be of any use. Every employee should receive the handbook upon hiring, and you should have a document for them to sign that indicates they have received, read, and understood the employee handbook. This document should be kept in their employee file.

Keep copies of the employee handbook where all employees can access it easily, whether in paper form or a digital copy. And then, when an issue arises, follow your own handbook.

Periodically review your employee handbook to make sure it is still accurate and relevant for your business. If you find employees are asking you a question repeatedly and that you haven't addressed it in your employee handbook, it might be a point that needs clarification.

CHAPTER 3

The Ultimate Guide To Finding Great Employees

Inside every great company is a great set of people who help run various aspects of the company, from administration to technical support. Choosing the right employees for your company can ensure a positive and productive environment in which everyone loves their job. In this chapter, we're going to look at how you can find great employees for your company.

Brainstorm the Ideal Candidate

Before you can find the ideal candidate for your current job opening, you need to define them. While their skills, experience, and education are obviously important, those shouldn't be the only traits you are defining. Here are some questions to ask yourself to come up with your ideal candidate persona.

• What skills must the ideal candidate have? These should be skills that your candidate must have when they walk through the door as opposed to something you would have to train or educate them to do.

• What skills would you like the ideal candidate to have in addition to the required skills they must have? These should be skills that would be a perk, but you could train or educate them to do them after you hire them if needed.

• Do you require the ideal candidate to have work experience using the skills required for their position? If so, how much?

- At what level would you prefer the ideal candidate's work experience using the skills required for their position? Think about whether you be comfortable hiring someone who was an intern or whether you are looking for someone who has had years of experience using the skills required for their position.

- In what industry or vertical would you prefer or require the ideal candidate to have work experience? Does your ideal candidate need to be in the same vertical or industry as your company or as your clients'?

- Do you want your ideal candidate to be someone that can ultimately move up the ladder? Think about whether they should be satisfied in the position you hire them for or should they have an interest in moving to a position of more responsibility.

- What educational background must the ideal candidate have? Keep in mind that someone with a specific degree is not automatically best suited for a job, and someone without one could have the experience on the job to make up for a college education. Also remember that certain recent certifications can demonstrate more relevance to your current job opening than a ten-year-old degree.

- What personality should the ideal candidate have? Should they be a team player because their job would require them to work with a team? Should they have the qualities of a good leader because you would want them eventually to become the manager of their department? Should they be self-motivated because they will be working in a department of one? Think of the type of personality you would want in your current job opening, and what type of personality would be needed to grow with your company. Then, you will be more likely to find someone who fits with your company long-term.

Once you have answered these questions, you will be able to identify the ideal candidate for your current job opening based on the information they supply on their resume. These answers will also help you define a better set of interview questions when you do choose the top applications. But before you write up that job listing…

Look Within

Why hire from the outside when you might have the ideal candidate sitting in your offices already? One of the top reasons people leave their jobs is because they are not given the opportunity for advancement.

You should start by announcing your new job opening within your company. You can do it openly from the beginning to give everyone a chance to show interest, or let the people you think are most qualified know about it first. If you do promote someone from within, you can also take advantage of having the person you promote train the person who will fill the position they are leaving. If you are not able to hire from within…

Write a Great Job Listing

Take the ideal candidate persona you defined in the first step and create a job description to match. Start by being as specific as possible. If you don't get a lot of applications, then you might want to consider broadening your horizons. But if you start specific, you might get the ideal candidate you want right from the start.

Be sure to put your job listing on your website. This way, you can start by sharing it to your social circles without having to pay fees for job listing sites. In addition to defining your ideal candidate, be sure to include the following in your job listing.

Offer Great Perks

On top of offering a competitive salary, perks can separate your company from your competitors who might be eyeballing the same ideal candidate as you are. Forbes listed some of the top perks of 2014 as game rooms, great food on campus, gym memberships, on-site yoga classes, time off, company retreats, child care, pet sitting, and other freebies.

When considering new perks to offer for your employees, start by deciding what perks you can offer, and then survey your current employees to find out which ones they would find the most valuable.

Advertise to Your Ideal Candidates

If you want to skip the job listing sites and only show your job ad to your ideal candidates, try paid social advertising. LinkedIn Ads, for starters, allows you to define your ad audience with highly specific criteria such as location, company, industry, job title, job function, seniority, school, field of study, degree, skills, and LinkedIn group membership. As you can see, you can easily narrow down your ad audience to fit the characteristics you defined for your ideal candidate.

Facebook Ads also offers some similar targeting options, including education level, field of study, employers, industry, job title, office type, and interests. To maximize your advertising budget, start by being as specific as possible. If you do not get responses, then you can broaden your search, but by being specific, you will spend less money for a more relevant audience.

Ask Unique Interview Questions

Using your ideal candidate persona, skip over the mundane interview questions and aim to ask specific ones. Give your ideal candidate examples of situations they might find themselves in and ask how they would handle them. Ask them how they would utilize their skill set to solve a particular problem. Gauge their interest in moving up the latter or staying put in the same position for a long time. Find out what their future goals are. Determine their personality type. With the right set of interview questions, you can learn more about your potential hires to make sure they will be the right fit for your company.

Give Your Employees a Chance to Interview

Remember that you are not the only person who is going to work with a new hire. Find out if other employees who will be working with your new hire are interested in being a part of the interview process. The ideal situation would be to get everyone on your new hire's future team to participate in a second interview where they can determine whether the candidate is a good fit. This second interview can help ensure that your new hire will not only do their job, but also fit well with the company culture.

If you follow the above steps, you are going to find great employees to become part of your company! They will be the type of employees that you will want to keep for years and years to come.

CHAPTER 4

Employee Benefits: Everything You Need To Know To Stay Competitive

Scrimping on employee benefits isn't the way save a few bucks.

Employee benefits are more than just the standard healthcare/ retirement package. They are the carrot in front of the horse, both enticing and keeping great employees on your team. They can make you stand out in a crowded and competitive industry.

In other words, employee benefits are part of how your business stays competitive.

The Law: Required Employee Benefits

There are some employee benefits that are not an option. If you have employees, you must provide the following benefits as required by law:

Social Security taxes. You must pay the same rate of taxes as your employees.

Unemployment insurance. Some businesses will be required to register with the state workforce agency where your business is located, and to pay unemployment insurance.

Worker's compensation. You must have worker's compensation insurance, whether you choose a commercial carrier, pay for it yourself, or through your state's program.

Disability insurance. Not all states require disability insurance, but you should check to be sure if you are required to help pay for a percentage of wages for sickness or injury off the job.

Leave benefits. Employers must honor the *Family and Medical Leave Act*, though they may offer additional leave above and beyond that such as for jury duty, military service, and other types of leave.

Best approach? Consult an expert to make sure that you are meeting your legal requirements. According to *Entrepreneur.com*, one of the most common mistakes that businesses make in this area is not giving benefits to all of their employees. Employers often fail to include part-timers when they should, or exclude custodial or clerical staff that they don't consider a "major" part of their team.

You can't be competitive if you aren't even meeting the law. So get this part right first.

Your Choice: Optional Employee Benefits

As long as you meet the law's requirements, you are under no obligation to provide any additional employee benefits. But, as I pointed out, you definitely will want to offer employee benefits above and beyond the bare minimum if you want to compete both in finding and keeping great employees. Some of the optional benefits might include:

- Retirement plans (including matching contributions)
- Vision and dental insurance
- Life insurance
- Paid vacation, holidays, or sick leave (the more generous the better).
- Health insurance (depending upon how the Affordable Care Act affects your business, it may not be optional).
- Regular pay raises, or performance or project bonuses (particularly important to provide incentives for employees who won't have an opportunity for promotion).

These optional items may vary according to the laws of your state or country, but they are considered standard in some industries.

Trends: Unusual Employee Benefit Trends

Employee benefits have changed significantly in the startup age. If there was ever a competitive industry, it's in the development and technology fields. Potential workers are no longer just weighing the salary, but they're considering the benefits with about as much equal weight.

Food and drink. On site meals, beer on tap — you name it. Providing serious food and snacks is a great perk, particularly for an office setting where your team puts in long hours and the workplace is their second home.

Health opportunities. Paying for gym fees isn't all that unusual, but having a climbing wall or exercise class right there at work is a whole new level of dedication to healthy employees. Some employers start small, paying for wearable fitness bands (like the FitBit) and reward employees for being active.

Entertainment. Game rooms, video games, music rooms — anything that encourages your team to take a break during the middle of the day and kick back for a bit.

Continued education. Helping your employees continue their education or further their skills tells them you think highly of them. Whether it's paying for college classes, conferences, group retreats, paid travel experiences, offering sabbaticals, or providing a yearly book allowance, a well-educated employee is a confident one, and a huge asset to you.

Freebies. Who doesn't like freebies? Employers give away everything from free products, subscription services, and daycare services.

But, according to Kate Harrison, contributor to Forbes, the most common employee benefit amidst all of these unusual trends is not so unusual at all: more time off.

In fact, some companies reward employees with a financial bonus if they take their time off (some even require them to disconnect completely), seeing great value in their team taking a break from the work environment and completely disconnecting.

Others have implemented a four-day workweek, either all year around, or seasonal (e.g. during the summer). According to Inc.com, a sense of renewal and improved creativity often happens when you allow employees more time off.

The takeaway from this is that you don't have to break the bank and build a full workout gym or install a bar in your office. Give your employees a chance to enjoy their life by giving them back their life.

Build A Competitive Edge With Employee Benefits

Some companies who use a broker or outside provider to help them with benefits go as far as using benchmarks to know if the employee benefits they offer are competitive or within industry standards.

How do you know which employee benefits you should have?

Follow the law. Make sure you are following the letter of the law and providing the benefits that the law requires. You'll probably even want to provide some of the more typical benefits even if the law doesn't require it. These are the benefits that employees expect. Not having them would make your business look poorly in comparison.

Consider your industry. Look at your industry and see what others are offering, and then determine what you could add that would make sense in your industry while setting you apart. First, find out what kinds of benefits your competitors are offering. Are you on par with what they provide? You should at least be offering that "bare minimum" in your industry. Then, consider what your industry requires. Is your's an industry that is quickly changing? You will want employees that are current in education and experience, and so offering educational benefits would make sense.

Consider your team. Once you have benefits that fulfill the law and compete at an industry level, you can narrow down benefits further and think of your specific team. Think about the team you have and the team you want. No two teams are alike, and they may have different preferences for what kinds of benefits and perks they'd like.

What will help make your workplace culture healthy and attractive to the kind of workers you want? If you're trying to attract young families, you'll might consider paying for daycare. If your workers are mostly young and single, daycare might not be a big selling point.

Additionally, men and women don't always prefer the same kinds of benefits. A Monster.com survey indicated that women placed more importance on vacation time, while men placed higher value on performance-based bonuses.

Where your employees are at in their career (starting out, nearing the end), their gender, relationship status, income and debt levels — these can all affect what kinds of benefits they prefer.

The easiest way to know what you should offer your employees is to ask your qualified employees what they'd like. What would it take to keep them on your team, loyal and diehard employees, no matter what other salary offer came their way? What would make their life easier?

Remember, any business can offer a salary. It's the unique and tailored benefits package that makes you stand out.

Consider the cost. It won't help you much if you offer benefits that you can't afford. While the first two (law and industry standards) don't offer much leeway, the third does. If you can't afford that full-featured gym that your employees want built into the office, promising it won't do much good.

There are extra benefits that can come without much cost to your business. The four-day work week with longer days, allowing telecommuting or flexible hours — these will not impact your bottom line all that much and in the long run, may increase employee satisfaction. Really interpret what your employees tell you they want. Are they really asking for you to pay for a trip to the Caribbean, or are they indicating they want more freedom and personal life time back? Substitute a gym membership for a built-in gym. Cater a meal into the office periodically instead of building a cafeteria. Give your employees their time back to use as they see fit instead of paying for a one-year sabbatical.

Not everyone has millions in their budget for amazing perks. Find benefits that fit your budget and still address the core concerns of your team.

Why Bother With Employee Benefits?

All of this sounds like a heckuva lot of work and extra expense for something that seems rather peripheral to your business, possibly, but there's a real reason for it.

Employees expect it.
A survey of workers revealed what they consider to be important when it comes to employee benefits. The most important benefit was healthcare, at 32%. This was followed by vacation time, at 25%. Pay raises, performance bonuses, and a retirement plan followed closely behind. Additionally, the normalization of benefits — including the "exotic" and trendy versions — means that new generations of workers are being taught to expect it and weigh those benefits as almost equally as they would the salary you offer. If you've been

involved in the hiring of Millennial workers, you've no doubt been on the receiving end of questions about the benefits you offer.

Employees will stay.

A 2015 Aflac survey of employees discovered that a good benefit package will help find and keep great employees:

- 38% of small-business employees said improving the benefits package would keep them in their job
- 87% said a well-communicated benefits package would keep them in their job
- 57% said they would take a job with less pay if the benefits were better

Great benefits will keep an employee from leaving even if a better salary offer comes along. Salaries come and go, but fantastic benefits are hard to let go of.

The salary you offer is no longer enough. Employees want benefits. They consider that as part of the salary calculation when deciding on where to work and whether to stay. You've put time and money into your employees. Losing them to a competitor because someone else offered better benefits is a loss of money and talent that you cannot afford over time.

CHAPTER 5

12 Employee Onboarding Best Practices Every Business Owner Needs To Know

If you've ever started a new job, only to find the company totally unprepared for your arrival, you know how important onboarding is to the employee-employer relationship!

But proper onboarding isn't just about first impressions. Taking the time to plan out how new hires will be introduced into your company will affect their future performance, their ability to achieve stated goals and their overall satisfaction with their new positions.

To help you succeed in these respects, consider the following this onboarding process that will help new hires integrate quickly into your company:

Before the New Hire Starts Work

Create an agenda for your new employee's first week. It's much easier to plan this in advance than it is to come up with while the new team member is standing there in front of you. If you aren't sure what to include on this agenda, have reach out to the new hire's soon-to-be manager or other key coworkers to determine what's important. If you assign mentors or work buddies, this is a great time do that as well.

Create a comfortable work station for your new staff member. Nothing kills a new employee's confidence in the company faster than being assigned to a dirty, unorganized desk. Setting up the workstation in advance gives new hires their own "turf," helping them feel more relaxed and confident. Fill the desk with any supplies needed, and place important documents – such as an organizational chart, employee handbook and new hire enrollment paperwork – on the desk for the employee's review.

Provide new employees with a welcome gift. To help the new hire immediately feel like part of the team, place any branded materials you offer on the desk, such as a custom t-shirt, a work bag, a coffee mug, pens, or a pad of paper. Not only will this build brand loyalty right away, it also helps a new employee feel welcomed.

Send out helpful information. Help soothe a new employee's first day jitters by clearly communicating any information that's needed for the first day. Include details on dress code, parking rules, directions to the office, and who to ask for when upon arrival to minimize new hire stress.

During The First Week

Help new hires get the lay of the land. On the new hire's first day, conduct a tour of the office. Be sure to include simple, but essential, information such as where their desk is located, where the restrooms and break room are, and where to find the copier and employee mailboxes. Introduce the new employee to other staff members along the way and encourage questions as you go.

Block off time for orientation. If you're in desperate need of help, it can be tempting to throw your new employee into projects as quickly as possible. But doing so can be disorienting and nerve-wracking – two feelings you definitely want to avoid! If possible, use the new hire's first day as more of an orientation day than a work day. Try to have some current team members take the new employee out for lunch, and set aside time for filling out paperwork, introductory meetings, and casual conversation.

Plan a manager's meeting. Sometime during the first week, set aside time for the new hire to meet with their immediate manager. Use this meeting to give the manager time to get to know the new team member, share their management style, and explain future expectations. It can also be helpful to use this time to let the new employee know what the ramp-up process will be like in the first month or two on the job.

Cover important work processes. As the new hire's first week progresses, have the new employee and manager meet a few more times as needed to discuss important work processes. For example, new staff members need to know email protocol, communication expectations, and internal decision-making processes. This is also a great time to set short term and long term goals. If the new hire will take on a supervisory role, they should also meet with their direct reports to begin to build rapport.

The First 30–90 Days

Invest in training. Though the productivity losses can be frustrating, a new hire's first 30-90 days on the job should be looked at as an initial training period. Train your new employee on everything from the ins and outs of your product line to your brand's positioning in the market. Once this introductory period is up, you'll have a much stronger worker than one you threw immediately to the wolves.

Allow for job shadowing. One of the best ways to train your new hires is to have them shadow other workers. But don't just focus on those in the employee's department. Cross training your workers by having them shadow employees in every department of your company will give them a much better understanding of how your organization works.

Build opportunities for feedback into the employee's first couple of months on the job. Make sure new hires know that they're free to share and encourage new ideas. They may not be comfortable doing so the first day, but over time, their feedback and insights should be encouraged.

Conduct your first review. Finally, after 90 days on the job, the manager should give the new hire their first evaluation. At this point, the new employee should be fully integrated into the company and operating at a full workload. Identifying weaknesses at this stage will allow you to either nip potential problems in the bud or terminate the new hire's employment before too many resources have been invested in an employee that won't ultimately work out.

CHAPTER 6

The Complete Guide To Employee Development

Ever hear the phrase "if you're not growing, you're dying?"

When it comes to our careers, this simple maxim is truer than ever. If we're not moving forward in our roles as leaders, managers, and individual contributors, it's impossible to get excited or motivated.

It's easy to get wrapped up in your own career advancement, but as a manager, you have to be invested in the career development of employees who report to you. What are their hopes and dreams? What do they hope to accomplish? What skills do they hope to gain before moving up within the company, or before moving on to a new role somewhere else?

It can be difficult to talk candidly about an employee's career goals, especially if those goals are not achievable within your organization. Even so, you should strive to take employees as far as they can go. It's up to you to foster the development of your employees.

In this chapter, I'll share everything there is to know about employee development, so you can make sure you're doing your job as a leader and manager:

Why Develop Employees?

As a manager, you need to work to develop employees, otherwise you're not doing your job, putting your career at risk.

"The number one reason employees quit their jobs is because of a poor quality relationship with their direct manager," said Monique Valcour in the Harvard Business Review. "No one wants to work for a boss who doesn't take an interest in their development, doesn't help them deepen their skills and learn new ones, and doesn't validate their contributions."

Valcour goes on to say that leaders should reward managers that make strides in employee development, and fire those that don't. Employee development not only results in individual improvement in quality and efficiency, but it also leads to greater retention and more motivated employees.

"Work groups in which employees report that their supervisor (or someone else at work) cares about them as a person, talks to them about their career progress, encourages their development, and provides opportunities to learn and grow have lower turnover, higher sales growth, better productivity, and better customer loyalty than work groups in which employees report that these developmental elements are scarce," said Valcour.

Leaders are taking notice of the managers who prioritize employee development. It's sink or swim– you don't want to be left behind.

Get on Their Side

If you want to develop your employees, you have to understand them. How to do this? Ask, and then listen.

We praise listening all the time, but most of us don't actually do it. Listening is a rare quality, but when it's done right, it can lead to fantastic results.

As a manager, you need to ask employees for feedback, and deliberately listen to their answers. Ask specific questions about certain projects to learn how they feel:

- How did you feel the collaboration went on our most recent project?
- Is there anything I could've done differently to make the process smoother?
- If we do this again, what would you recommend we do differently?
- What aspects of your job do you enjoy most? Are there any areas where you'd like to improve?

When employees answer with suggestions for how a process could be done better, or frustrations with how something is going, you need to listen carefully. If an employee feels as though they've been heard, they'll know that you're on their side.

Remember that your job is to help employees help themselves. Micro-management is a real problem, and you need to be carefully to listen carefully, and grant autonomy so that your employees feel that they're in control of their own destinies.

Work Together to Help Determine Career Goals

In order to excel at developing an employee, you need to work with them to determine their goals, then work towards them.

The Human Resources department at University of California at Berkeley recommends working with your direct report to write an Individual Development Plan, usually known as an IDP. In this model, the manager is responsible for encouraging, supporting, removing obstacles, and providing resources so that the individual can make strides in their professional development.

Here is what the HR department at Berkeley suggests for a plan of action:

- Meet with your direct report to discuss their plan and goals
- Provide feedback on their goals
- Provide suggestions for activities that can help them reach their goals
- Help them set realistic timelines for goal achievement
- Help them troubleshoot potential obstacles

- Schedule meetings to check in and see how they're doing
- Remain flexible and revise plan as needed

Whether you use this strategy or not, you should find a way to support employee development in your organization.

Help Find Strategies and Tools to Reach Goals

Once you and your employee have created an IDP, you need to help them reach the goals they set forward.

Although employees have the best intentions, they often struggle to reach their goals because they are unclear on expectations, lack organizational skills, and have difficulty creating realistic time frames. Software, productivity strategies, and personality assessments can help employees work more efficiently, helping them reach their goals.

Software
Software tools aren't a catch-all solution, but they can certainly provide help and direction for employees, improving efficiency by making it easy to schedule and collaborate. Here are some tools to consider:

- Project management tools like *Trello* and *Basecamp* make it easy to plan out projects and coordinate with team members.
- Calendars and scheduling software like *When I Work*, *Calendly*, and *Smartsheet* make it easy to create timelines and schedules.

- Job-specific software like *HubSpot* for content marketers and *QuickBooks* for accountants can increase productivity, especially for small teams.

Productivity Strategies

There are tons of articles on productivity, but you need to find strategies that work well for your employees. Here are some common tactics that can help employees develop and reach their goals:

- Deadlines may seem like an old school tactic, but they work! Dan Ariely, best-selling author, swears by deadlines, even if they're self-imposed.
- Daily and weekly routines help ground employees. What tasks need to be done every day? Maybe an employee can spend the last hour of their day or shift doing a certain task, ensuring it gets done in a productive fashion.
- Check-ins and meetings help remind an employee that you're on their side and have their best interests in mind. Make sure to check in on how an employee is doing when it comes to goals and productivity on a weekly basis.

Professional Assessments

Professional assessments may seem hokey, but they're helpful tools that can help employees better understand themselves. These assessments will also help you understand their motivations so you can better support them. Here are some of my favorite professional assessment tests:

- Myers-Briggs categorizes everyone into 1 of 16 personality types, then gives results to help test takers understand strengths and weaknesses in their personal and professional lives. You and your employees can take the tests for free at http://16personalities.com.
- DiSC personal assessment profiles helps people understand how they interact with others in the workplace so they can improve their communication style to build more productive teams. Learn more at https://www.discprofile.com/what-is-disc/overview/.
- Other personality tests

Connect Employees to The Company

One of the ways that employees develop and grow is if they feel connected to the company's initiatives. If they feel that their work is helping the bottomline, driving success, and is valued in the organization, then they'll be more motivated. Here's how to foster that spirit:

- Promote internal social networks so that employees feel connected to co-workers, even if they're in different departments.
- Loop employees in on company-wide initiatives so they always feel connected and never feel like they're out of the inner circle. Your openness will encourage them to be more open.
- Find opportunities for cross-collaboration so that employees get exposed to how different aspects of the business work.

Granting Autonomy to Help Employees Develop

Think acting like a helicopter boss will help employees? Think again. Empowering workers and giving them autonomy reduces employee turnover, according to a study conducted at Cornell University.

The researchers studied 320 companies and found that roughly half granted employees a lot of autonomy and freedom. It turns out that these businesses grew 4x more than those with rigid rules and traditional hierarchical structures. As a manager, you need to find ways to make your employees feel as though they're in control. They should be creating their goals, not you. They should have some say over which tools they use and which strategies they employ to get their jobs done.

It pays to give autonomy, so don't micro-manage.

Employee Development for a Better Organization

Investing in employee development will reduce turnover, increase motivation, and ultimately make your organization more productive and efficient. If you follow the tips in this chapter, you'll be well on your way to developing employees that go on to have fabulous career.

CHAPTER 7

A Quick Guide To Effective Employee Engagement

You wouldn't be a company if you didn't have employees. And, if you want to be successful in business, you need employees who are effective, engaged, and excited to contribute.

But how can you get your employees engaged? It's not as simple as throwing a big party and asking employees to get pumped up about their projects. Employees are engaged when they feel fulfilled by their work, are well supported by the company and their team, and feel they are contributing to the company's goals.

If employees feel like their main job is to grind out work, why would they feel engaged? As a business owner or manager, it's your job to make them feel at home.

You can prioritize employee engagement by getting everyone on the same page, building a culture that puts employees first, and implementing company-wide programming that has engagement at its core.

Why Does Employee Engagement Matter?

You didn't hire your employees because they're great at ping pong. You hired them because they have skills you need to be successful.

But skills are one part of the puzzle. Disengaged employees are expensive– in 2012, Gallup found that low employee engagement could cost the U.S. economy about $370 million every year.

Not only are disengaged employees costing you money, but their counterparts result in higher profits, safer work environments, and increased productivity. Gallup's study found that engaged employees have 37 percent lower absenteeism, 48 percent fewer safety incidents, 21 percent higher productivity, and 22 percent higher profitability.

The proof is in the pudding.

Get Everyone on The Same Page

Sure, employee engagement is something you want, but how do you get it?

To improve employee engagement, you need everyone on the same page. You need general agreement that employee engagement is important, which means buy in from leadership and middle management. If the company leaders are not engaged, it will be impossible to spread engagement through the rest of the company.

Even if some aren't super psyched about spending resources and money improving employee engagement, make sure leaders know about any changes that will be happening. For most initiatives, they should be clued in before their staff.

But being on the same page is about more than getting employee engagement initiatives through– it also means making sure that everyone at the company understands the values and the culture that you're trying to build. It means that people are aware of company goals.

You don't need to change your entire business model to facilitate awareness– even monthly and quarterly emails can do a lot to clue people in. Just make sure they're well-written, as transparent as possible, and interesting to read.

There are two main steps to effective employee engagement:

Step 1 – Build a culture that prioritizes employees.
Step 2 – Implement company-wide programming that reflects the culture.

Step 1. Build a Culture that Prioritizes Employees

Your company culture needs to prioritize employees– there's no other way to get effective employee engagement. Here's how:

Create Values, and Live by Them

"Do as I say, not as I do" is a maxim that never works well on children. Well, it doesn't work well on employees either. You can't just tell employees to be engaged. Instead, you need to create a culture where the status quo is engagement, and you can do that by creating a company mission and set of core values.

For example, FreshBooks uses the acronym PORCHFEST as a shorthand to describe its values to employees— these values are Passion, Ownership, Results, Change, Honesty, Fun, Empathy, Striving, and Trust.

Countless employees have core values like FreshBooks does, and these values not only help employees understand expectations, but they also help hiring managers make better choices. These core values function as standards for hiring. If a prospective candidate can't live and breathe the company values, then they're probably not worth hiring.

Give Good and Fair Benefits

People work because it's fulfilling, but they also work to provide for themselves and their families. They care deeply about how much money they make, what benefits they get, and how flexible their work environment is.

It's in your best interest to provide good and fair benefits to employees. Good benefits increase employee retention, which in turn saves you money.

If you don't have a major budget, think of creative ways to offer benefits. Maybe you can't offer the world's most competitive salaries, but you can offer equity. Maybe you can't offer health insurance that covers everything, but you can get creative by offering HSA or FSA accounts.

Invest in Professional Development

There's a famous saying about investing in employees: an executive says "why should we invest in our employees? what if they leave?." Another employee looks right at him and says "what if we don't, and they stay?"

The point? Investing in professional development is good for your employees– and for the business.

Conferences, online courses, master's degrees– opportunities abound on and offline for further learning and professional development. There are online courses on leadership, marketing, and business development for reasonable prices.Intelligent.ly offers leadership courses, while General Assembly and Udemy offer courses of all kinds.

Larger conferences are more expensive, but they're also a great way for employees to learn.

Reward for Good Work

When employees do work hard and get results, recognize them for it. It's easy for employees to lose motivation if they're not getting any benefit from working hard. Why be engaged if the company doesn't show its appreciation?

Company-wide recognition and awards are important, as are raises and promotions. Make sure you have quarterly meetings to assess performance. Simple things like office high fives go a long way, as do company-wide emails highlighting accomplishments.

Be careful not to play favorites– constant recognition of one employee over and over again can frustrate employees, too.

Step 2. Implement Company-wide Programming

Once you've built a company culture that prioritizes employee, you need to implement company-wide programming that ensures your core values are followed. Here's how:

Company Events & Outings

Company events and outings have been around forever, but there's more to it than hosting a holiday party where everyone drinks a lot. Employees need to kick back and have fun, but they also need to feel they serve a greater purpose.

You need a healthy mix of professional events (such as monthly lunch and learns, and quarterly meetings), organized social events (such as go-kart racing, boat cruises, cocktail parties), and charity events (such as 5k races, charity walks, and other volunteer events).

Bringing people together for shared activities will help everyone get on the same page, and allow them to interact in ways that differ from their day to day routine.

Gifts for New Hires and Major Events

Gifts are a thoughtful way to express your appreciation and excitement. That's why hiring managers honor new hires with personal gifts. After you've made a hire, send a thoughtful gift to their home before they start. This will make them feel welcome and excited before they even step through the office doors.

Send gifts when major life events occur, too. If someone buys a house, gets married, has a child, finishes a degree program, or gets terribly sick, make sure to send something their way. It doesn't have to be big– it's the thought that counts.

If you're unsure what gifts to give, Small Business Trends put together a great list of clever employee gifts that can be used year-round.

Employee-to-Employee Recognition

Employee-to-employee recognition programs take employee engagement out of the hands of leadership, and drop it in the lap of the employees.

Zappos is famous for their employee-to-employee recognition programs– they have four of them! Employees can nominate colleagues for covered parking spots (it's hot in Vegas) by writing up a story of how they helped out. They can earn zollars, a Zappos currency, by volunteering to help out.

Come up with a creative way to encourage employees to recognize each other. Prizes don't hurt!

Employee Engagement Matters

You're a great manager, but you can't get employee engagement by yourself. Creating effective employee engagement is no easy matter, but ultimately, it will save the business money and make your company a great place to work.

Let your employees personalities shine– and give them opportunities for growth. If you follow the advice in this chapter, you'll be well on your way to improving employee engagement at your organization.

CHAPTER 8

How To Manage A Disgruntled Employee

We've all seen disgruntled employees. They're unmotivated, decline to join in on team activities, and don't seem to respect the company much. Perhaps they're amazing at what they do, or maybe the company can't afford to lose the employee. Often, a passionate employee loses some of their gusto, suddenly becoming a disgruntled employee who is difficult to deal with.

No matter the circumstances, your job as a manager is to deal with disgruntled employees. In this chapter, I'll show you how.

What Does It Mean to be Disgruntled?

The dictionary defines disgruntled as displeased and discontented; sulky; peevish. Eek. Doesn't sound like a quality most managers want.

When we have these employees in our workplaces, they're detrimental to our company cultures. They spread negative energy, promote complaining, and encourage others to forget about getting things done.

If others see that you permit employees to be disgruntled, they're a lot more likely to become disgruntled themselves. It's essential to nip these problems in the bud for the good of your company.

Signs an Employee is Disgruntled

Many managers ignore the obvious, tell-tale signs that employees aren't motivated, or worse, about to quit. After all, it's painful to see an unhappy employee under your change. Part of your job is sniffing out the signs, even if you don't want to see them. How can you help a disgruntled employee if you don't know they're unhappy?

Here are some obvious signs that your employee is disgruntled:

• Lack of motivation, excitement, or passion
• Showing up late, taking long lunches
• Not participating in meetings
• Talks about projects and the company in a negative way
• Dresses up and leaves the office (possibly going on interviews)
• Has gone through a recent personal crisis
• Other people in the office are frustrated with the employee

Find Out WHY Your Employee Isn't Happy

Once you've determined you've got a disgruntled employee on your hands, you need to figure out why. Learning the reason is the only way you can fix the problem.

There are many, many reasons employees can become unhappy– some may be directly related to the office, while others may have little to do with it. Some reasons are more problematic than others, but most are fixable, as long as you understand what the real problem is. To learn why an employee is unhappy, **ask, and actually listen to their answers.**

Don't corner the employee in a room and complain to them about how they aren't living up to your expectations. Instead, say: "I've noticed you seem a bit spacey lately. Is something going on?." If that leads you no where, try: "I've noticed the quality of your work is suffering, and I am very concerned. Do you have any idea why this is happening?"

This is a potentially stressful conversation, and we highly recommend reading Harvard Business Review's *Taking The Stress Out of Stressful Conversations* before having a meeting about performance concerns. Employees often get defensive if you approach the topic wrong, and this resource has great suggestions for having a positive, game-changing conversation, even when it's stressful.

Once you've assessed what's bothering the employee— whether it be a lack of challenge, a personal problem, or conflicts with colleagues— you'll be better able to help. Don't forget to document these conversations and their results so that you can cite them later, if need be.

Decide If It's About Them or You

When things go wrong, it's easy to blame the employee. "She's not getting anything done," you say. "He keeps complaining about our vacation policy." Are you providing a positive work environment for your employees? Maybe you think you are, but are you really? Usually, it takes two to tango, so it's not helpful to blame the employee for their lack of productivity.

Maybe they are struggling with productivity because they're unclear on what your expectations are, or maybe they don't have a good project management system in place. As a manager, you can change both of those things.

But sometimes, it might be more about the employee than about the company and the systems you have in place. If you've worked to change everything, and the employee is still unmotivated, dissatisfied, and disgruntled, it might be time to let them go.

Be Professional Along The Way

Disgruntled employees make us angry. Here we are working our butts off, only to have an employee that can't get anything done, and doesn't seem to care. But we can't let this anger and frustration get the best of us.

OpenFORUM recommends five steps for managers dealing with these types of employees: Remain professional, don't let it fester, keep it private, document everything, and don't empower them.

At the heart of OpenFORUM's recommendations is professionalism. Don't let the situation fester without doing anything– this doesn't help anyone. Make sure to keep matters private so they don't create extra gossip in the office. Document everything so that you can keep track of warnings, especially if you choose to fire the employee later.

Change Behavior with Good Management Strategies

Great managers can turn things around by employing good strategies. There are two main steps to dealing with a disgruntled employee:

• Listen to them
• Come up with solutions

If you are able to listen and understand the problems an employee is having, and work with them to come up with real, game-changing solutions, you've done your job as a manager. Of course, there are strategies that can help you listen and understand better– don't bombard an employee with questions. Ask one, and wait for an answer, even if you're sitting in silence for a little while.

You can come up with helpful solutions, too, by really getting at the heart of the matter. Try helping the employee set up a new task management software solution, a better calendar, or encourage them to work on a project with a colleague they really like. Put systems in place to help prevent them from falling through the cracks.

If an employee can't rise to the occasion after that, it might be time to think about letting them go.

Be Ready to Let Go

If an employee is causing you grief, you might have to make the difficult decision to let them go. At some point, the disadvantages will begin to outweigh the benefits, and it may be time to say goodbye.

Firing is not easy to do, so make sure you've taken notes along the way, and that you've given the employee warnings about the consequences of their actions. It's not fair to fire someone if you haven't given them a chance to rise to the occasion. If you feel as though you've worked tirelessly to help, and it's just not working out, it's better for both to move on.

Sometimes, a company just isn't a great fit for an employee, and that employee isn't a great fit for the company.

Building a Culture Without the Disgruntled

Even the best company cultures have disgruntled employees, but it's on you and your company's leadership to build a culture that doesn't have room for disgruntled employees. How to do this? Invest deeply in building out a company culture, creating values and a mission that prevent you from hiring these types of people in the first place.

Values such as honesty, integrity, and generosity will quickly weed out employees who won't fit in. Writing these values down will help you to assess prospective employees whenever you interview them.

Don't be afraid to fire disgruntled employees that show no signs of turning things around, either. This is your company we're talking about– you want the best employees on the planet.

CHAPTER 9

How To Fire An Employee: Everything You Need To Know

Did you know that the way you handle an employee's termination is often the deciding factor in that person's decision to sue you or not?

There are lots of ways to handle firing someone, but very few of us know which way is the best way. It's an emotional situation, which not only affects the person being fired but also your business and your entire team. This is why terminating someone makes it extremely difficult to lead with your intellect instead of your emotions.

Fortunately for you, we have personal insights and conducted in-depth research on workplace termination. We're going to share what we learned and how to fire an employee in the best and most compassionate way possible – in a way that will not make them want to retaliate against you.

In this chapter, I broke down the firing process into three phases: before, during and after. Then I provide you with tips, warnings and a handy dandy checklist to ensure you do this right.

Before

Make a plan. Before you ever hire someone, you should have a plan in place to fire them – a termination letter and complete documentation will be required. This sounds horrible, but it's the best thing to do for everyone.

Action item: Write a list of reasons why an employee would ever be fired. Turn it into a cohesive, easy-to-digest document. Share it with new hires so they know what you expect at the very minimum from everyone on your team.

Define the role. The next document you should have is clearly defined list of employees' responsibilities and key performance indicators (KPIs), i.e. the items or metrics you're judging them on.

Action item: Sit down with current and new employees, and go over these expectations of positions' documents with each person individually. Give them monthly goals to hit and monthly performance reviews so everyone knows where they stand with you.

Document religiously. The very first time and each time after that, issues with employees should be documented and dated. Of course, it is best to email this person the issue(s) at hand so you leave a paper trail, and they can have ample amount of time to digest and improve.

Action items:
- When a problem is noticed, first email your employee and then set up an in-person meeting to discuss it.
- In the meeting, be nimble. Try to get to the root of the problem, and see what could be the cause behind their poor performance.
- Focus on the facts, adding zero comments or opinions.

- Outline specific improvements that must occur by a certain date. Possibly create a project plan to help get them back on track.
- Ask what you can do to help them improve their performance.

Be Transparent. It is pertinent to be completely transparent with employees, who are on the road to termination.

Action item: Clearly state the next step is termination if x, y and z is not done, completed, improved and/or met by a specific date. Don't beat around the bush. Use the word "termination."

Prepare. Once you know you're going to fire someone, it's time to make another plan. One that answers the following questions:

- How will your team function without this employee?
- Will you hire or reassign their work to another employee?
- Will or should I provide them with severance?
- How and when will I share this information with my team and the person?
- Where will you tell him or her?
- What questions may they ask me?
- What is my reasoning(s) for firing them?

Action item: Answer the questions listed above and any others that may pop up in the meantime. These should be easy to answer if you've been transparent with your employee as we recommended in the aforementioned steps.

During

This is the hardest part – actually telling someone they are no longer employed. It can be absolutely painful and definitely emotional.

This is why it's pertinent to not torture them with small talk, but rather just lay the blow within the first 30 seconds of being in the room.

Action items:
- State your case and the reason for it.
- Do not drag things out. All of the details should have been previously discussed in prior meetings, which led up to this.
- Spit it out. Don't torture them.
- Concisely explain the details of the termination.
  - Remind them of any legally binding agreements they initially signed with the company, such as NDAs, confidentiality agreements, etc.
  - Tell them how and when they can pick up their belongings.
  - Collect company collateral.
  - Allow them to take any legal documents you want them to sign home to review.
  - Include any details about severance packages, benefits, health insurance, etc.

- Consider offering complementary services if the person is genuinely a good person, but just wasn't right for this particular job. This could include:
  - Recommendation letter for their soft skills
  - Simply thanking them for what they did do
- Answer any questions they have professionally and concisely.
- Be prepared for emotions.

After

Whew. That was tough. Now, all you have to do is break it to your staff and monitor your reputation for the time being.

Tell your employees. Don't embarrass the former employee because chances are they have friends in the company. Consider letting people know on a need-to-know basis or by simply stating in the next meeting that so-and-so will no longer be working with us.

In order to protect the privacy and legal rights of your former employee, be careful about how much information you give to your current employees about the termination. Your goal should be to keep people informed enough so that they can continue being effective in their own roles, so that they understand relevant workplace rules and guidelines, and to prevent any potentially damaging rumors from spreading.

Monitor. In today's socially connected world of the Internet, it's important to set up tools to monitor what a potentially disgruntled ex-employee might be saying about you.

Action item:
- Set up Google Alerts to get notified immediately when something pops up for your company's name.

That's essentially it. This is the high level bullet points of what we believe you should do when you need to fire someone. One last thing though – let's talk legalities.

Legalities

Regardless of whether or not you've handled everything the right way, you still may have an upset ex-employee on your hands; therefore, it's important to know what you need to do to stay within the law.

Here are five answers to the most frequently asked questions surrounding employee rights and the law.

1. **What is the Employment at Will Policy?**
   According to the *Small Business Administration*, every state except Montana allows employers the option to create an "at-will" employment policy. This means you can let someone go at any time during employment, without explanation, at any time.

2. **When is it illegal to fire an employee?**
   You cannot fire someone for the following reasons:

- Discrimination, i.e. firing based on race, gender, religion or disability
- Whistleblowing, i.e. firing for speaking up about the company's illegal activities, health and safety violations or discrimination or harassment (This reason does vary by state)
- Legal requirements, i.e. firing for taking medical, military or family leave or taking time off for jury duty or to vote

3. **What benefits are your employees legally entitled to if they are fired or terminated?**
   Employees may be entitled to the following benefits upon termination:

   - Health insurance coverage continuation
   - Unemployment insurance
   - Vested retirement plans

4. **Am I required to immediately give the employee their final paycheck?**
   No, you are not required by federal law to immediately compensate your former employee, but some states do require so check with a lawyer to be certain. The state will be specific about what should be included in that final paycheck.

5. **Am I required to offer severance?**

   The Fair Labor Standards Act does not require you to provide severance pay.

CHAPTER 10

How To Battle Employee Turnover

If you believe that your employees are your biggest resource, then you know the damage high employee turnover does to your business. The time and money you've invested in finding, hiring, and training employees walks right out your door when an employee quits.

How to battle employee turnover?

It starts with an understanding of why employees leave. Until you know their reasons, there is little you can do to stop the leak.

Why Do Employees Leave?

Employees leave a business for a lot of different reasons. Most of these reasons are under your control, even in a roundabout way.

Better wages and benefits found elsewhere.

Both hourly and salaried employees are tempted to leave if a better wage or benefit package is found elsewhere. In fact, dissatisfaction with wages is the top reason salaried employees leave. Hourly employees, especially, may be tempted by even a slightly higher wage elsewhere. This is particularly true if they have no benefits. It's easy to walk away and get a better wage when there's so little to lose.

Additionally, if employees think that the business is not financially secure or that there is an impending problem in the leadership, they may bail ship before anything happens.

Bored with the work.

Employees who are bored will quit.

Not enough work to do. Assignments that are no longer a challenge but are merely rote habit. No chance to use skills and abilities that might fall outside of a strict job description. No sense that they can self-assess and decide what to do because of rigid management that doesn't allow for it.

These are all reasons employees get bored.

Trouble in the team.

Not everyone is easy to get along with, and even the best matched team will have personality clashes on off days. But serious and ongoing conflict in the workplace costs you a great deal of money.

A recent study found that American employees spend 2.8 hours each week dealing with conflict. That's time you're paying them that they aren't working for you. 25% of employees say that conflict causes them to be sick or absent from work. Anger and discord spill across the whole team and will eventually make its way to the customer, affecting sales. And, employees will quit to be free from all of the negativity.

They are disengaged.

Employee disengagement is extremely common. As in, 70% of American workers are all but elsewhere when they should be working, according to a recent Gallup poll. Once employees disengage and turn work into merely a time clock and a paycheck, businesses will see 30% to 50% higher turnover.

Engaged employees are productive, innovative, creative…"sick" less often. Disengaged employees have little incentive to be any of those things, and quick to find the door. When your employees feel like they're just the tool to be used so someone else can achieve their dream or financial success, they disengage.

Poor relationship with the boss.

Are you the problem?

A recent study suggests that half of employees quit because of problems with their boss. A bad boss is one that:

- Overloads and makes excessive demands on employees, burning them out.
- Micro-manages everything they do.
- Is hard to reach, is rarely around and not working their own business, or otherwise difficult to talk to.

- Has no idea how bad hiring, promotions, and other employee-related decisions are upsetting those already on staff.
- Cares more about him or herself than the staff, making all decisions based on what he or she wants.
- Holds terrible meetings, and wastes employee time.
- Is unable to communicate where the company is going, or where the employee's job and career might be going.
- Unable to perform successful conflict resolution within the team.

A bad boss ruins the work situation all across the board. Employees can put up with a lot, but a bad boss is the limit.

How To Keep Your Employees From Leaving

How do you think you stand up next to your competitors, in the eyes of your employee? Your competitors aren't just the others in your industry, but any job that the employee could leave you to take.

One of the best things you can do is get an exit interview with an employee, if the situation allows. This isn't the time to be defensive or combative, but genuinely ask why they are leaving. You may need to revamp your business in several key areas.

Offer great benefits.

Making a great wage and salary available is only part of it. Your benefits package is, at this point, almost considered part of the wage. Even for hourly employees, you can offer benefits. Benefits, after all, aren't only relegated to medical and retirement. They might include:

- Flexible hours and vacation time.
- Gift cards when team or individual milestones are met.
- Free food or beverages in the break room.
- Pay for employee training such as conferences, books, online classes, or part of an employee's college fees.

Benefits can be the hook that keeps an employee, particularly if they are benefits not easily or comparatively found elsewhere.

Have great culture.

There are two kinds of culture at play in your business: internal and external. The first is what your employees experience, and the latter is what your customers see your business as. Great internal culture is more than just a ping pong table and casual clothes.

Not every workplace is well-situated for that modern version on work culture (e.g. your employees may be required to wear uniforms), and not all employees even want that. In fact, many employees actually prefer a more structured and traditional hierarchic order where there are levels of management. Each type of business has a different type of culture inherent to its industry.

Whatever culture you have in your place of business, and whatever management structures you have, your internal culture is less about the games and free beer and most importantly about safety, trust, and reliability. Any workplace that makes an employee feel fearful, defensive, or always on edge is one they'll leave.

External culture matters, to, particularly to millennials who want to work for a company that is doing good things in the world. Employees like to know that they work for a company that stands for something bigger than the job itself.

To make your culture work, you have to communicate to your employees what it is. That will include both practical and abstract concepts such as:

Benefits. The wage and other benefits that will be given to all employees.

Expectations. What you expect of everyone on the team, including management.

Rules. The behavior limitations that make the work environment safe for all. This includes conflict resolution policies.

Rewards. The possibility of promotion, bonuses, wage increase, and anything that gives a sense that there is a tangible reason to work hard.

Core Values. The freedoms, value of input, the value of the team, and the reason an employee should stay engaged.

Much of this will be reflected in your employee handbook and, of course, how well you follow-up and actually run your business according to it.

Acknowledge great work.

Letting your employees know they've done a great job is paramount. They want and need feedback on how they are doing, especially millennials. A generic approach to recognizing a valuable employee, though, isn't really the greatest approach. Consider customizing that recognition depending upon the situation. The *Robert Half blog* suggests a few ideas:

• Email the employee, and CC his or her manager.
• Send a written card or note.
• Tell them in person.
• Give a gift, such as a gift card to a local restaurant.
• Throw a small party, even if it's just in the break room or a get-together after work.
• Return the favor and help them back.

Exceptional work and behavior that goes above and beyond

what you expect should see the larger reward, but don't forget to commend, in some small way, employees who are chugging along and meeting your expectations. Knowing that their work is appreciate is what helps them keep going.

If your employee does well, let her know. If she keeps doing well, provide a tangible reward.

Be upfront about the job.

35% of American workers quit in the first six months. When the post-hire reality sets in, it might not be what employees expected. No one advertises a job, it seems, without a little sugar-coating.

When new employees are told to expect a certain culture, a particular manager, specific benefits or set of perks, and then realizes that won't happen, they are quick to turn to the idea of quitting and cutting their losses before getting in too deep.

Even if you are desperate to hire someone for a position, you must not oversell the position or the culture of the workplace. Ask the potential employee questions that get to the bottom of what they are hoping for from the job. UPS asks potential hires if they are looking for full-time work (they'll probably be disappointed if they are). Wells Fargo has employees watch real videos of difficult and angry customer transactions so the potential hire can see if they really want the job.

Deal with conflicts immediately.

Conflict in your team will decimate your culture and the entire work environment. As mentioned previously, your customers will even get a taste of it and will think of your business as one to avoid because the employees are unpleasant. The truth is simple: a conflict-free business is one both employees and customers want to be at.

Dealing with conflict isn't easy, but there are a few approaches:

• Learn to identify conflict. Most conflicts start small, with actions that managers might not even notice. Subtle bullying and harassment, such as purposefully ignoring someone or giving them a look, can be the small start of something huge.

• Meet in private. Bring the conflicted employees together in private. Talk in private and slow, deliberate tones. Everything about this meeting is to listen and ascertain what is happening, and to keep things from escalating.

• Help them understand. In the meeting, let each take a turn explaining their point of view. Before the other can speak, they must restate what the other point of view is to the coworker's satisfaction. This is to help all parties understand what the other is feeling and get past their own complaints.

• Stick with it. No one leaves until their is a resolution. The resolution must be genuine, even if it involves the exit of an employee for good.

- Don't be afraid of throwing the bad apple. For the sake of the rest of your employees, it is better to get rid of one (or two) who is causing problems than let the rest be spoiled.

There are some leadership personalities that thrive on conflict, but most people don't. Definitely don't get the mistaken idea that constant conflict is "good" for the team and encourages creative competitiveness. You're working a business, not a fight arena.

Hire the right people for the right job.
Above all, hire the right people.

Great workers are not the right worker for every job. The best employee will be miserable in a job poorly matched to skills, abilities, and personality.

Why do managers do this?

They mistake skills for talent and interest. They ignore the importance of a person's attitude and focus on the work they can do. They think lower level jobs are easy and insignificant, sorely missing the point about how important the person working the sales floor directly with customers truly is. Or, that proper training will fix any poor employee-job match. Even worse, they first look to family and friends.

Perhaps the best thing you can do to stave off employees turnover is to make sure you hire the right employee in the first place. While you cannot completely control what happens in an employee's life and the decisions they'll make, you can at least make every attempt to make their work situation positive.

CHAPTER 11

How To Train Your Employees To Become Managers

Where do you find the perfect manager? Hiring a manager from within your current employees seems wise. Who better knows your business that those already working it?

Managing, though, is a special kind of leadership. It can be challenging to be the middleman between the employees and the owner.

Unfortunately, in many small businesses, formal management training is rare. If employees show themselves to be good workers, they get promoted whether they are ready to manage or not. Rather than plucking employees from their current job and dropping them cold turkey directly into management, you can begin training your employees to be managers right where they're at in their current job.

The basic principle to making this approach work is to consider the qualities of a good manager, and then provide employees the opportunity to build those qualities now. Management skills can be broken down into three basic areas, according to leadership expert Eric Basu:

1. **Personal skills.** This is the ability of an employee to evaluate themselves and identify strengths and weaknesses.

2. **Team-focused skills.** This is the ability of an employee to manage, motivate, and communicate with small groups.

3. **Corporate skills.** These are the skills and drive to make your business more successful.

Having all three of these skills are necessary for every manager. So how do you go about growing these three key skills in your employees?

Create A Culture Of Learning

First and foremost, create a culture of learning. By doing this, you create employees who aren't satisfied unless they are always pushing themselves and meeting new challenges. Management requires a person who is bent towards learning, always wanting to find the best way or the new technology to make things work better.

1. **Training is more than job-specific.** Offering your employees training for their specific job is the most obvious way to approach learning in the work place. However, this tends to be a short-sighted solution because it leaves you with employees who are perfectly trained for a specific job — they might know how to run a machine or work with customers — but do not know anything beyond what their job requires.

Training, in general, is more than just learning to operate a cash register. According to Business Insider, training has the potential to increase productivity and improve employee retention, for starters. Even Starbucks realizes this, offering their employees a chance to earn a college degree by helping them do it. Giving your employees the chance to learn more than they need to empowers them on the job.

Start seeing training for what it does beyond the knowledge it provides.

2. **Help employees learn how to learn.** Even if your employees want to learn about things that aren't immediately related to their job, encouraging a culture of learning, no matter what they learn, is the key. Knowing how to learn is its own skill, one a manager must have as they face different situations that they will need to quickly understand and disseminate.

Let your employees practice the art of learning through training.

3. **Training doesn't have to be expensive.** Entrepreneur Richard Branson is known for encouraging lifelong learning in his employees. Branson is wise to point out that providing this training doesn't necessarily mean huge expense. Author Mary K. Pratt echoes this sentiment in regards to affordable training, outlining six creative and low-cost ways you can encourage learning.

If you can't offer training in house, provide incentives for employees to learn on their own. Give them a book allowance, or time off to attend conferences. Pay for online courses or encourage them to use free options like Coursera. Reward employees if they complete online courses or certifications.

Whether you bring a trainer in or use access to online courses, the promise of training is both an incentive for employees and way to build key skills in your future managers. Investing time and money into training your employees also makes a clear statement on how valuable they are.

Encourage Time Management Techniques

Managers of people are also managers of time, and helping your employees learn to use their own time wisely now will embed time management principles that will help them later, when they are a manager.

Delegation. Teach your employees to break their job down into smaller tasks. In a sense, they are learning how to delegate their time to themselves to be more productive. When they become manager, they are able to delegate tasks to other people in the same way.

Prioritization. Help your employees learn to discern which tasks are the most important and must be done first, and which can wait until later. You might start by prioritizing their tasks for them and explaining why you have ordered them in this manner. As time goes on, let them prioritize tasks on their own.

Goal setting. Goals can be as small as not taking a personal call during working hours, or as large as getting all the new stock on the shelves by the end of the shift. They might be number-based productivity goals or more overt time management goals.

Again, you might start by setting a few benchmarks for employees and then eventually give them the freedom to make their own goals. In meetings or employee reviews, ask about the daily, weekly, and personal goals they have set for themselves and what they are doing to meet them.

Build Team Communication Skills

Helping your employees learn to communicate with other employees before being asked to manage them is a huge component. Communication, after all, is one of those things that, once broken, can lead to horrendous problems.

1. **Make your team meetings work double time.** You likely have regular meetings, whether the whole team is assembled or a shift crew. Turn these meetings into a communication exercise by having employees take turns leading the full meeting, or at least part of it.

Squeeze some communication training into a meeting with something as simple as showing a TED talk or quick SlideShare presentation. Have a suggestion box and feature one question or suggestion to discuss each meeting. Let your employees get real-world practice with communication by keeping your meetings from being a one-sided top-down lecture and encouraging them to lead the discussion.

2. **Familiarize employees with your company's jargon.** Jargon and industry terminology aren't just for the people making the decisions. They are a key component to understanding what happens inside your business.

Let all of your employees in on the words and phrases used so that when they hear you use them, they understand the context, they know what you are talking about, and they don't feel like management is keeping them in the dark. Encourage them to use the technical terms of your business. It's better that they all learn it now rather than have to practically learn a new language when they are promoted to management.

Encourage The Practice Of Leadership

Becoming a manager without leadership skills is a recipe for disaster. By helping your employees to see themselves as leaders no matter what their position or whether or not they even work full-time, you instill an understanding of what leadership entails. Leadership should already be in place when the promotion to being a manager comes along.

1. **Leadership happens in the small things.** Honesty, following company policy, and obeying rules are those small things that many workers fudge a bit here and there because "it isn't really hurting anyone." Leadership in the small things points to how an employee will handle the bigger things, however.

   Does your employee consistently arrive a bit late for his shift? Does your employee fail to follow a dress code once in a while? Maybe "borrow" supplies, or give their friends a discount at the cash register? Then he is not ready to lead, because he cannot yet lead by action.

   Again, those seemingly unimportant things are an indicator that there is something big beneath the surface: the employee either doesn't respect your business, your goals, or your leadership enough. And that is someone who isn't ready to be a manager.

To help employees understand that the small things matter, address this kind of "small" behavior (in private) the first time you see it so that it doesn't have a chance to become a habit.

This is your chance to help them understand what it takes to lead: actions matter more than talk. It goes without saying that you, as the leader, should be also leading by example in caring about these "small" things, or you'll have an impossible time demanding it of your employees and future managers.

2. **Create low-level leadership opportunities.** Leading others is a scary proposition, particularly for employees who have never done anything like it before. In order to make the process easier, start by creating "low-level" practice opportunities.

Do you have shift managers? Can you rotate employees to take turns at some aspect of managing a shift or typical work day? Can you assign someone the task of scheduling and leading a meeting? Planning the front window display?

When considering how to delegate tasks that need to get done, consider that leadership opportunities are part of that delegation.

Pull Back The Curtain And Reveal The Big Picture

Helping your employees understand your business better is part of building their corporate skills, one of those three key areas of leadership.

1. **Build better attitudes about employee value.**
    Employees can easily get into the mindset that the management doesn't really want them to understand the bigger picture, and so their only responsibility is to clock in and do the job they were assigned.

    That kind of attitude doesn't work for a manager, and to help keep it from even setting in, it's best to let your employees understand how they fit into the larger plan.

    Tell your employees what the goals are that their work will be involved in. Even your part-time employees need to know they have a valuable place in that plan. The employee at the cash register isn't just ringing up sales. She's the face of the business to customers. Help her see how she fits into a larger picture.

    Seeing where and how they fit provides them the chance, if their attitude allows it, to see beyond the narrow "that's not my job" mentality and instead go out of their way to see that things get done. At that point, employees are more like management material. They have the larger goal in mind, and see where the smaller pieces fit.

2. **Help them understand success affects them.** A decent employee is motivated to get their own paycheck, and so she does the work you tell her to do, but isn't terribly motivated to do much more. After all, she's here to get paid and that's it.

A great employee wants to see the business succeed because he knows that it also means he will succeed. He goes above and beyond, because getting paid isn't his only motivation. He wants to be part of a success.

The second employee is going to help your business grow. They will care about loss prevention, lost sales, dissatisfied customers, and all of those daily things that affect your bottom line. The best way employees can understand how success affects them is to let them get a reward when your business reaches a success milestone.

From something as small as a catered meal after a big sale to a pay increase when sales goals are met, directly reaping the benefits of your business's success motivates employees to make it happen again. If your business relies on your employees to be the success it is, not letting them share in the reward de-motivates them completely.

Whether your business is retail, service, or staffed mainly

by part-time employees, these methods can — and should — be put into practice. It is easy for hourly employees, whose pay is measured by the time they give to you, to slip into the mindset of clocking in and clocking out. That mindset does not make a good manager.

By giving your employees the chance to build management skills and habits before they become managers, you are making it possible to easily see which employees will actually make the best manager. You are, essentially, seeing them use their skills in a "sandbox", before they are actually needed.

CHAPTER 12

How To Measure And Boost Employee Satisfaction

Whether it's with a summer vacation, a new dress, or a job, people care about having experiences that satisfy them. Everyone wants to be satisfied.

As a leader or manager, you want satisfied employees, people who are excited to come to work, motivated to do a good job, and open to changes and collaboration. Satisfied employees are:

- Happier, more content, and more motivated at work.
- Generally more productive.
- Better able to collaborate with colleagues.
- More likely to positively spread the word about your organization as brand advocates.
- More likely to stay at your organization for a long time, reducing employee churn.

Ultimately, satisfied employees give back to your company, making it grow into the best place it can be.

But how do you measure employee satisfaction? How do you know if the critiques that comes from your employees are serious signs they're dissatisfied, or if they're standard run-of-the-mill suggestions?

And once you've figured out how you're doing, how can you make improvements? You not only want to ensure your employees are satisfied, but you want to improve their experiences at your company as time goes by.

In this chapter, I'll explain how you can measure employee satisfaction, as well show you can boost it.

How to Measure

If you're able to measure employee satisfaction, you'll be able to understand where you can improve, and in what areas you're lacking.

One-on-One Conversations

Imagine you work for an organization with 40 people. It's unrealistic to expect that you'll get one-on-one time with them naturally. So, schedule one-on-one conversations. Many companies have these types of conversations on a weekly, monthly, or quarterly basis. Be clear about the goals of these sessions. Ultimately, you want to find out about how satisfied the employee is with their roles and the company as a whole. When you enter into one of these conversations, don't go with an agenda. Come up with a series of questions to ask the employees, then listen to their answers. Here are some good questions to ask employees in a one-on-one meeting?

- What are some things you think we're doing well?
- What aren't we doing well?
- If you could change one aspect of your job, what would it be?
- What do you wish you were doing more of?

- Do you think the team is successful at working together? Why or why not?
- Do you see yourself here in five years? Why or why not?

Record what they say. You can ask employees to clarify what they mean, but don't get defensive if they say something you don't agree with.

Surveys

Sometimes it's difficult for employees to express themselves to their leader or manager, especially if they are concerned about how the other party will take it. That's why surveys, especially anonymous ones, can be helpful tools. Surveys also help you get quantitative data, rather than just a bunch of ideas and suggestions.

For example, if you ask employees if they feel generally satisfied with their job, you'll get a percentage who say they are, and a percentage who'll say they aren't. These percentages will help you gage how you're doing instantly.

To conduct a survey, use *SurveyMonkey, Google Forms, TinyPulse, 15Five*, or any survey tool and send it to everyone in the company. Make sure you can make the surveys anonymous, so that employees will be as honest as possible about their feelings.

Read Between the Lines

Sometimes, the satisfaction of your employees won't be completely obvious, so it's your job to read between the lines. Even if you have the best intentions, one-on-one conversations might go no where. Employees might be intimidated by your position of leadership.

Do some research and learn about salaries in your area to see if what you're offering is competitive. If you're paying below market rate, your employees know that. They're probably not satisfied with their pay, and could be looking for new opportunities, or simply feeling bad.

Talk to friends outside the office and ask them what they're biggest issues at their jobs are, to see if you're having any similar issues at your own offices. Talk to other leaders at your company to see what they think— are their employees satisfied? What could be done to improve?

How to Boost

Once you've measured current satisfaction at your company, you can start working to improve it. Here's how:

Attack the Real Issues

A satisfied employee is happy with their workplace as a whole, so you won't get anywhere if you solve the problems with bandaids. Many managers see that their employees are less than satisfied, and they try out sudden, sweeping gestures, in the hopes that employees will see how much they care. Unfortunately, a fun party or a spontaneous pizza party aren't going to suddenly make your employees satisfied.

Instead, you need to attack the real issues your employees are having, even though they're probably hard to fix. If employees feel overworked, you have to find a way to create a more balanced workload. If employees feel underpaid, you have to figure out a plan to increase salaries.

If Necessary, Make Big Changes

I once had a friend who worked for an organization that paid all of its writers pennies to write thousands upon thousands of words per day. Problems in employee satisfaction weren't going to be solved by a small raise or a minor cut in word count. In order for this organization to thrive, leaders would've had to make large changes in how they conduct business. They would've had to bring in a business consultant to set them on the right path, and change the way they structured jobs.

Employees can get on fine without snacks and parties, but they suffer when they feel they are undervalued, underpaid, and overworked. You may need to make large changes to improve employee satisfaction. Don't be afraid to take risks to make it happen.

Bring in a Consultant

You're a leader, not a mind reader, and you're so wrapped up in your organization that it can be difficult for you to see how you can improve. Organizational psychologists and executive coaches can see things you can't– that's why it's worth calling them up.

These psychologists and coaches can lead workshops and sessions, take surveys, and help you come up with a plan for improvement. Coaches can come with a price tag– a Harvard Business Review survey of coaches said the average hourly rate is $500– but many coaches are satisfied with the results.

Harvard Business Review also offers advice on what to look for in a coach, based on what those who've hired coaches say. Sixty-five percent recommend hiring a coach or psychologist that has experience coaching in a similar setting.

Keep it Light

No one likes to feel like they're in trouble. Just because you're trying to improve a big issue like satisfaction doesn't mean you need to make it heavy and confrontational. Sometimes, when you ask employees tough questions, they can get defensive and worry that their jobs are in danger. Remind your employees that you're doing this so you can create a better place to work, and that their honesty and participation will make the process easier, and ultimately result in a better work environment for them.

Employee Satisfaction Builds a Great Company

How can you build a great, profitable organization if your employees don't like coming to work? As a leader and manager, it's on you to work to improve employee satisfaction. If you're able to do so, you'll create a more productive workplace, reduce employee churn, and ultimately build a better, stronger company.

Conclusion

The road to management doesn't stop once you move into a leadership role. It's an ongoing process that requires constant attention, effort, enthusiasm, and motivation.

I hope the concepts and ideas covered in this book have sparked in you a desire to become a better manager and leader of your team.

If you have questions or comments on anything in this book, please contact me:

Email: c.halvorson@wheniwork.com
Twitter: @ChadWorks or @WhenIWork
Facebook: facebook.com/wheniwork
Website: wheniwork.com

For even more tips and tricks on how to become a better manager, check out our blog at wheniwork.com/blog.

We're constantly publishing fresh content aimed at helping you improve your business, build a better team, and become a better leader.

Thanks again for reading!

Chad Halvorson

CEO of When I Work

55662516R00070